INSPIRATIONS

A personal collection of poems, proverbs and quotations

Written and compiled by Derek Dobson

Published by
Runnymede Publishing
173 Widmore Road
Bromley
Kent BR1 3AX

Phone: 020 8460 1215
Fax: 020 8460 0999

ISBN: 0 9524486 0 2

· A NOTE FROM THE AUTHOR ·

I have put together this small collection in the hope that it may bring some consolation to those who are experiencing great sadness in their life, and to others as a way of reflecting on a current problem which needs resolving.

Words alone will never be enough, but they can help considerably. The very thought that you are not alone – many others feel the same – can contribute to the healing process. The path of recovery is long and hard but a few sincere and meaningful words might help you reach the end of what seems like a never-ending journey. This is especially true if you are experiencing a bereavement – so often painful beyond belief. Only you know how it feels, and sympathetic friends can reveal an innocent naivety in what they say. They mean well but sometimes do not know how to handle such situations.

To the others of you who are looking for inspiration and strength, I hope you find a few words of comfort to see you on your way.

Finally, to anyone who has some words of their own and would like to contribute to another book, please feel free to send them to me for consideration. We all need inspiration at times.

DEREK DOBSON

"If I had my life to live over again, I would have made a rule to read some poetry and listen to some music at least once a week; for perhaps the parts of my brain now atrophied would thus have been kept active through use.

The loss of these tastes is a loss of happiness, and may possibly be injurious to the intellect, and more probably to the moral character, by enfeebling the emotional part of our nature."

CHARLES DARWIN (1809 – 1882)

Death is but a door,
through which we all must pass.
Do not fear or ask for more,
for there you will find the
green green grass.

DD

My first poem and dedicated to
my sister Freda (R-in-P 22.9.1983)

· FOR THOSE IN DOUBT ·

Have confidence in yourself to do
what you think is right.
Fear not what others might say.
Press ahead with determination and dignity.
Strive with all the energy you have.
Ignore criticism from those who cannot see.
Have the strength to pursue your vision.
And in the end you will achieve your goal.
For what is right will succeed.
It is then that others will learn from what
you have done, and make it all worthwhile.

DD

We value most that which we have lost.

DD

There is a time for everything,
and a season for every activity under heaven:
a time to be born and a time to die,
a time to plant and a time to uproot,
a time to kill and a time to heal,
a time to tear down and a time to build,
a time to weep and a time to laugh,
a time to mourn and a time to dance,
a time to scatter stones and a time to gather them,
a time to embrace and a time to refrain,
a time to search and a time to give up,
a time to keep and a time to throw away,
a time to tear and a time to mend,
a time to be silent and a time to speak,
a time to love and a time to hate,
a time for war and a time for peace.

ECCLESIASTES 3 v 1-8

Memory is the yesterday
that gives us courage
for tomorrow.

ANON

· THE NEXT ROOM ·

Death is nothing at all. I have only slipped away into the next room. I am I, and you are you. Whatever we were to each other, that we still are. Call me by my old familiar name, speak to me in the easy way which you always used. Put no difference in your tone, wear no forced air of solemnity or sorrow. Laugh as we always laughed at the little jokes we enjoyed together. Pray, smile, think of me — let my name be ever the household word that it always was, let it be spoken without effect, without the trace of a shadow on it. Life means all that it ever meant. It is the same as it ever was, there is unbroken continuity. Why should I be out of mind because I am out of sight? I am waiting for you, for an interval, somewhere very near, just round the corner. All is well.

CANON HENRY SCOTT HOLLAND (1847 – 1918)

Don't let other people's faults
be an excuse for your own.

DD

· TAKE TIME ·

Take time to think
it is the source of power.

Take time to play
it is the secret of perpetual youth.

Take time to read
it is the greatest power on earth.

Take time to love and be loved
it is a God-given privilege.

Take time to be friendly
it is the road to happiness.

Take time to laugh
it is the music of the soul.

Take time to give
it is too short a day to be selfish.

Take time to work
it is the price of success.

Take time to do charity
it is the key to heaven.

ANON

· THE SERENITY PRAYER ·

*God grant me
the serenity to
accept the things
I cannot change,
courage to change
the things I can,
and wisdom
to know the
difference.*

ANON

*If we could start life with
the knowledge with which we end it,
how much better this world
would be!*

DD

· LOVE IS EVERYWHERE ·

Love is a funny thing to describe. It's so easy to feel and yet so slippery to talk about. It's like a bar of soap in the bathtub — you have it in your hand until you hold on too tight.

Some people spend their lives looking for love outside themselves. They think they have to grasp it in order to have it. But love slips away like that wet bar of soap.

Holding on to love is not wrong, but you need to learn to hold it lightly, caressingly. Let it fly when it wants; when it's allowed to be free, love is what makes life alive, joyful and new.

It's like the juice and energy that motivates my music, my dancing, everything. As long as love is in my heart it's everywhere.

VICTORIA GAIFORD

Learn from what you did yesterday,
live today to the full and
leave tomorrow to take care of itself.

DD

· FROM WHENCE I CAME ·

How lonely life can be
when people cannot talk to me.
Am I just an empty shell,
or could this place be living hell?

If I had a voice,
could God give me a choice?
I've read the book of Psalms
in the hope He'll take me in His arms.

Now I've left this place called Earth,
where I have lived since birth.
My Maker bids me welcome.
How safe and warm I feel.

DD

Dedicated to Ernie (R-in-P 12.12.1989)
who suffered from senile dementia.

Be strong and courageous.
Do not be terrified;
do not be discouraged,
for the Lord your God will
be with you wherever you go.

JOSHUA 1 v 9

· THROUGH GRIEF ·

There is no way round grief, only a way through.
Grief cannot be hurried.
You need time to mourn and accept tragedy.
Grief and bereavement come to us all.
You will find it impossible to accept.
You cannot believe it has happened to you.
You yearn for them.
Grief is the price of love and being loved.
And you must grieve – you need to release your feelings.
It is natural to cry and sob.
As natural as smiling and laughing.
Do not deny or hide your grief – accept it.
It is a healing process, a way of coming to terms with loss.
Let your tears and feelings come.
Do not bottle them up.
Crying is not self pity – it is a necessity – so cry when you need to.
Eventually you will come through that long, dark tunnel.

DD

To keep your head out of the clouds,
keep your feet on the ground.

DD

· PRAYER OF ST. FRANCIS OF ASSISI ·

Lord, make me an instrument
of Thy peace;
where there is hatred, let me sow love;
where there is injury, pardon;
where there is doubt, faith;
where there is despair, hope;
where there is darkness, light;
and where there is sadness, joy.
O Divine Master, grant that
I may not so much seek
to be consoled as to console;
to be understood as to understand;
to be loved, as to love;
for it is in giving that we receive,
it is in pardoning that we
are pardoned, and it is in dying
that we are born to eternal life.

If there be just cause
then rest assured I will pursue it.
If there be not, then I will pause...
...and figure out another way!

DD

· LIFE – PART 1 ·

Life is like the seasons.
Spring brings the birth.
Flowers break through the earth
from their seeds below,
Summer brings the sun to help them grow.
The occasional shower will make them weep
but also gives them strength to seep.
With autumn the stems begin to bend,
for they cannot live for ever.
Winter comes with bitterness and snow,
for surely it is time for them to go.
But no!
The leaves may wither, shrivel and die,
but the roots remain –
to live again in God's domain.

DD

· A GRATEFUL MESSAGE FROM AN AGED PARENT ·

Blessed are they who understand my
faltering step and shaking hand.

Blessed are they who know my ears
today must strain to catch the things they say.

Blessed are they who see; to know my
eyes are dim, my mind is slow.

Blessed are they with cheery smile who
stop to chat for a little while.

Blessed are they who make it known:
I'm loved, respected and not alone.

GLADYS MAY REEVES

*Anybody who looks down on you
is not worth looking up to.*

DD

Life is so very precious,
it hangs by a thread from above.
If only God would let us
hold on with all His love.

DD

Dedicated to 'Carrie'
(R-in-P 9.8.1988)

Do not be quick with your mouth,
do not be hasty in your heart
to utter anything before God.

God is in heaven
and you are on earth,
so let your words be few.

As a dream comes when there are
many cares,
so the speech of a fool when there
are many words.

ECCLESIASTES 5 v 2-3

· A POPPY TO REMEMBER ·

I picked a Poppy in Flanders today,
It was growing alone in the long thick grass
With a strong determination to live come what may,
One of what was many, but this the last.

The same can be said of lives that were lost
in a war that was not worth their terrible cost.
For what happened in Flanders was an obscenity to those left behind,
Of men that were, but one of a kind.

Tombstones by the thousand, many but boys,
Used by the 'Powers' as simple decoys.
Those brave young men, who gave their today for our tomorrow,
What would they give for a life to borrow?

A life, a life, so much to live for,
Snuffed out in a second by a single shot.
What was theirs to come is no more
and now their bodies are left to rot.

What is to be of mankind, if we have come thus far
after two thousand years and a bright yellow star?
God give us the courage to stand up and fight
and bring back some sanity from out of His light.

So let that Poppy be a reminder,
To help me remember those gallant young men.
Its colour appropriate in the hope we become kinder,
A crimson red, like the blood they shed.

DD

A wise man has knowledge,
a lucky man has love.

DD

Charity begins where it is needed.

DD

· WHAT IS DYING? ·

A ship sails and I stand
watching till she fades on the
horizon, and someone at my
side says, "She is gone".
Gone where? Gone from my
sight, that is all; she is just as
large as when I saw her...
The diminished size and total
loss of sight is in me, not in
her, and just at the moment
when someone at my side
says "she is gone", there are
others who are watching her
coming, and other voices
take up a glad shout, "there
she comes!" ...and that is
dying.

BISHOP BRENT

· LOVE – PART 1 ·

And now I will show you the most excellent way.

If I speak in the tongues of men and of angels, but have not love, I am only a resounding gong or a clanging cymbal. If I have the gift of prophecy and can fathom all mysteries and all knowledge, and if I have a faith that can move mountains, but have not love, I am nothing. If I give all I possess to the poor and surrender my body to the flames, but have not love, I gain nothing.

Love is patient, love is kind. It does not envy, it does not boast, it is not proud. It is not rude, it is not self-seeking, it is not easily angered, it keeps no record of wrongs. Love does not delight in evil but rejoices with the truth. It always protects, always trusts, always hopes, always perseveres.

Love never fails. But where there are prophecies, they will cease; where there are tongues, they will be stilled; where there is knowledge, it will pass away. For we know in part and we prophesy in part, but when perfection comes, the imperfect disappears. When I was a child, I talked like a child, I thought like a child, I reasoned like a child. When I became a man, I put childish ways behind me.

Now we see but a poor reflection as in a mirror; then we shall see face to face. Now I know in part; then I shall know fully, even as I am fully known.

And now these three remain: faith, hope and love. But the greatest of these is love.

1 CORINTHIANS 13

Simplicity is genius

· LIFE – PART 2 ·

Life is about learning.
Through it we experience
the elation of happiness;
the depth of despair.
The strength of our character
is tested again and again.
Have we the courage to stand on our own?
Have we the determination to go on?
With God at our side
and a refusal to hide
Nothing can surely deny us.

DD

Never be afraid to do what is right.

DD

I live alone, dear Lord,
Stay by my side.
In all my daily needs
Be Thou my guide.
Grant me good health,
For that indeed, I pray,
To carry on my work
From day to day.
Keep pure my mind,
My thoughts, my every deed,
Let me be kind, unselfish
In my neighbour's need,
Spare me from fire, from flood
Malicious tongues,
From thieves, from fear,
And evil ones.
If sickness or an accident befall,
Then humbly, Lord, I pray,
Hear, Thou my call,
And when I'm feeling low,
Or in despair,
Lift up my heart
And help me in my prayer.
I live alone, dear Lord,
Yet have no fear,
Because I feel Your presence
Ever near.
ANON

When I was quite young, my grandmother taught me a Chinese proverb – or so she said it was – which had to be said aloud at all times of stress both good and bad. When everything was awful, dreadful or depressing you must use the phrase; when everything was wonderful and glorious and exciting you were to use the phrase. When everything was dreary, dull and boring you were to use the phrase – in fact you should say it at least once a day!

And the phrase? Just four words:

THIS TOO WILL PASS.

And my grandmother was right. I've used the phrase many, many times (if not every day!) and it never fails to get my wheels back on the rails.

CLAIRE RAYNER

Do not listen to what a person utters from his lips but read his eyes, for there you will find the truth.

DD

· FOOTPRINTS ·

One night I had a dream.
I dreamed I was walking along the beach with God and
across the sky flashed scenes from my life.
For each scene I noticed two sets of footprints
in the sand, one belonged to me and the other to God.

When the last scene of my life flashed before
us I looked back at the footprints in the sand.
I noticed that at times along the path of life
there was only one set of footprints.

I also noticed that it happened at the very
lowest and saddest times of my life. This really
bothered me and I questioned God about it.

"God, You said that once I decided to follow You,
You would walk with me all the way but I
noticed that during the most troublesome times
in my life there is only one set of footprints.
I don't understand why in times when I needed You
most, You would leave me."

God replied, "My precious, precious child,
I love you and I would never, never leave you
during your times of trials and suffering.

When you see only one set of footprints it was
then that I carried you."

ANON

It's nice to be important
but it's more important to be nice.

I heard this said by the ex football manager,
now commentator, Theo Foley, who was
quoting his mother.

The Lord is my shepherd; I shall not want.
He maketh me to lie down in green pastures:
He leadeth me beside the still waters.
He restoreth my soul: he leadeth me in
the paths of righteousness for his name's sake.
Yea, though I walk through the valley of the
shadow of death, I will fear no evil: for
thou art with me; thy rod and thy staff
they comfort me.
Thou preparest a table before me in the
presence of mine enemies: thou anointest my
head with oil; my cup runneth over.
Surely goodness and mercy shall follow me
all the days of my life: and I will dwell
in the house of the Lord for ever.

PSALM 23

*It's easy to follow but
not so easy to lead.*

DD

· DESIDERATA ·

Go placidly amid the noise and haste, and remember what peace there may be in silence. As far as possible without surrender be on good terms with all persons. Speak your truth quietly and clearly; and listen to others, even the dull and ignorant; they too have their story. Avoid loud and aggressive persons, they are vexatious to the spirit. If you compare yourself with others, you may become vain and bitter; for always there will be greater and lesser persons than yourself. Enjoy your achievements as well as your plans. Keep interested in your own career, however humble; it is a real possession in the changing fortunes of time. Exercise caution in your business affairs; for the world is full of trickery. But let this not blind you to what virtue there is; many persons strive for high ideals; and everywhere life is full of heroism. Be yourself. Especially do not feign affection. Neither be cynical about love; for in the face of all aridity and disenchantment it is perennial as the grass. Take kindly the counsel of the years, gracefully surrendering the things of youth. Nurture strength of spirit to shield you in sudden misfortune. But do not distress yourself with imaginings. Many fears are born of fatigue and loneliness. Beyond a wholesome discipline, be gentle with yourself. You are a child of the universe, no less than the trees and the stars; you have a right to be here. And whether or not it is clear to you, no doubt the universe is unfolding as it should. Therefore be at peace with God, whatever you conceive Him to be, and whatever your labours and aspirations, in the noisy confusion of life keep peace with your soul. With all its sham, drudgery and broken dreams, it is still a beautiful world. Be cheerful. Strive to be happy.

MAX EHRMANN (1872 – 1945). Written in 1927

Live today as though it were your last.
For tomorrow you may not wake up
....and discover it was.

DD

· 17th CENTURY NUN'S PRAYER ·

Lord Thou knowest better than I know myself that I am growing older and will some day be old. Keep me from the fatal habit of thinking I must say something on every subject and on every occasion. Release me from craving to straighten out everybody's affairs. Make me thoughtful but not moody: helpful but not bossy. With my vast store of wisdom, it seems a pity not to use it all, but Thou knowest Lord that I want a few friends at the end.

Keep my mind free from the recital of endless details; give me wings to get to the point. Seal my lips on my aches and pains. They are increasing, and love of rehearsing them is becoming sweeter as the years go by. I dare not ask for grace enough to enjoy the tales of others' pains, but help me to endure them with patience. I dare not ask for improved memory, but for a growing humility and a lessening cocksureness when my memory seems to clash with the memories of others. Teach me the glorious lesson that occasionally I may be mistaken.

Keep me reasonably sweet; I do not want to be a Saint — some of them are so hard to live with — but a sour old person is one of the crowning works of the devil. Give me the ability to see good things in unexpected places, and talents in unexpected people. And, give me, O Lord, the grace to tell them so. AMEN.

THE TITLE OF THIS PRAYER IS TRADITIONAL, THE SOURCE UNKNOWN

*Loneliness is running out
of things to think about.*

DD

· LIFE – PART 3 ·

Life is a gift from above
so cherish it with all your love.
Do not take it for always granted
or else you will become disappointed.

Treat each person as a friend
even if they're solemn hearted.
You may be able to help them mend
a soul that love's departed.

Why oh why do we sometimes cry?
Can it be just a lie?
Goodness no, it helps us smile
to make life all worthwhile.

DD

"Do not let your hearts be troubled.
Trust in God; trust also in me. In my
Father's house are many rooms; if it were
not so, I would have told you. I am going
there to prepare a place for you. And if
I go and prepare a place for you, I will
come back and take you to be with me that
you also may be where I am. You know the
way to the place where I am going."

Thomas said to him, "Lord, we don't know
where you are going, so how can we know
the way?"

Jesus answered, "I am the way and the truth
and the life. No one comes to the Father
except through me."

JOHN 14 v 1-6

The greater the pain,
the greater the reward.

DD

Your father's time has come to go,
Now that God has beckoned him so,
The door of life has opened wide,
To let him through and pass inside.

Who are we to say,
When and where we go?
It is not for us to choose,
Who we love or who we lose.

Before you shed a painful tear,
Whisper in his waiting ear,
"Farewell, my darling Dad,
Farewell, for all the love we've had."

DD

Dedicated to a father who was
loved and will never be forgotten.

· WORDS FROM AFAR OR JUST NEXT DOOR? ·

"If I could wish upon a star
and leave the door of life ajar.
How wonderful it would be,
to know you still love and cherish me."

DD

Words that may have been spoken by a
lovely, loving and loved man.
FRED (R-in-P 7.3.1990)

*If you look long and deep enough
there is normally something
positive in even the unhappiest
of situations.*

DD

Before I leave this earth
on which I have lived since birth,
let no word go unspoken or any deed
undone.

Treat each day as if it were your last,
for today will surely become the past.
If tomorrow doesn't come,
then regrets there will be none.

And when I'm gone from where I belong,
do not cry or feel all sad
for you will make me very mad!

Remember I'm just going next door,
to a place where there's so much more.
To a place that has been prepared
by Him above.
To a place that's full of love.
Oh my friends, it's Heaven above.

DD

Excuses do not alter facts.

DD

Love must be sincere. Hate what is evil; cling to what is good. Be devoted to one another in brotherly love. Honour one another above yourselves. Never be lacking in zeal, but keep your spiritual fervour, serving the Lord. Be joyful in hope, patient in affliction, faithful in prayer. Share with God's people who are in need. Practise hospitality.

Bless those who persecute you; bless and do not curse. Rejoice with those who rejoice; mourn with those who mourn. Live in harmony with one another. Do not be proud, but be willing to associate with people of low position. Do not be conceited.

Do not repay anyone evil for evil. Be careful to do what is right in the eyes of everybody. If it is possible, as far as it depends on you, live at peace with everyone. Do not take revenge, my friends, but leave room for God's wrath, for it is written: "It is mine to avenge; I will repay," says the Lord.

On the contrary: if your enemy is hungry, feed him; if he is thirsty, give him something to drink. In doing this, you will heap burning coals on his head. Do not be overcome by evil, but overcome evil with good.

ROMANS 12 v 9-21

A mistake made is a lesson learned.

DD

You can't enjoy smiles
if you haven't cried tears.

You can't feel good
if you haven't felt bad.

You can't appreciate life
if you haven't felt death.

And you can't be happy
if you haven't known love.

DD

For our time is a very
shadow that passeth away.

WISDOM 2 v 5

At moments of anguish and despair let
those who have been apart come together.

For at times like this we all need the
strength of friendship.

Let us put aside thoughts of jealousy,
anger and bitterness.

It is only with love, a shoulder to
cry on and each other that we will
come through our adversity.

Let us all hold out a hand.
Let us be friends.
Let us be happy.

DD

· JUST FIVE MINUTES TO SAY FAREWELL ·

Oh my love, my darling love,
Why did you leave me so soon?
You flew away on the wings of a dove
leaving my feelings wrapped up in a cocoon.

If only we had just five minutes more
I have so many things to say
They are kept in my heart not far away
So listen to me as you did before.

You gave me happiness that was beyond all belief
Whenever it came it was such a relief
I just looked into your eyes
and gone were my sighs.

Whenever I was in trouble
You were there at the double!
No ifs, no buts, no whys,
You simply held out a hand without any surprise.

When I felt low
and tried not to let it show
You just took one look
and read me like a book.

When I'm alone and in need of solace
I simply take out your picture and look at your face.
Back come the good times that we had together
Come rain, come shine no matter the weather.

When the children are in bed and all is still
I shed a tear and listen for your voice
I look through the window as I did before
I wait for your footsteps and a knock on the door.

Although I know you're not coming back
I have just one small wish that remains in my heart
Just five minutes more that's all I implore
Simply to say a few words and wish you farewell.

DD

When my time has come to go,
I pray to God I'll not say so...
If only I had....
What if I....
I wish....
I'll simply say....
.... I did.

DD

Tomorrow is too late.

RAY MOORE

*Different words mean different
things to different people.*

*Hopefully, you will have found a few
words that mean something to you.*

DEREK DOBSON

GRATEFUL ACKNOWLEDGEMENTS

Jon Stock

For helping with the
production of this book

Angie Thick

For assistance in the typing and
layout of the original manuscript

Pictor International

Cover photograph and page 24

Wilhelm Rauch

Remaining photographs

Claire Rayner

Contributor

Victoria Gaiford

Contributor

The Holy Bible

New International Version

And last, but certainly not least, the many
bereaved and courageous people to whom I have
spoken and who have provided me with the
'inspiration' to write many of my poems.

DEDICATED TO
My late sister FREDA